THE GREAT OUTDOORS

DEER HUNTING

Revised and Updated

by Randy Frahm

Consultant:
Lou Cornicelli
Big Game Program Coordinator
Minnesota Department of Natural Resources

3 1389 01894 0023

Capstone press®

Mankato, Minnesota

Edge Books are published by Capstone Press,
151 Good Counsel Drive, P.O. Box 669, Mankato, Minnesota 56002.
www.capstonepress.com

Library of Congress Cataloging-in-Publication Data
Frahm, Randy.
    Deer hunting / by Randy Frahm.—Rev. and updated.
    p. cm.—(Edge books. Great outdoors)
    Includes bibliographical references and index.
    ISBN-13: 978-1-4296-0817-6 (hardcover)
    ISBN-10: 1-4296-0817-X (hardcover)
    1. Deer hunting—Juvenile literature. I. Title. II. Series.
SK301.F64 2008
799.2'765—dc22   2007012249

Summary: Describes the equipment, skills, conservation issues, and safety concerns of
deer hunting.

Editorial Credits
Carrie A. Braulick, editor; Katy Kudela, photo researcher; Jenny Krueger, revised
edition editor; Thomas Emery, revised edition designer; Kyle Grenz, revised edition
production designer

Photo Credits
Capstone Press/Gary Sundermeyer, 11, 13, 25, 27, 35, 43; Gregg R. Andersen, 15,
    18, 22
Corel, 30 (all), 44, 45
iStockphoto/Soubrette, 32
Jeff Henry/Roche Jaune Pictures, Inc., 7, 38, 41
Mark Raycroft, 5, 8, 29, 37
Shutterstock/Mike Rogal, cover
Spomer/Hazelwood/Visuals Unlimited, 16
Unicorn Stock Photos/Ted Rose, 21

1 2 3 4 5 6 12 11 10 09 08 07

TABLE OF CONTENTS

Chapter 1 Deer Hunting 4

Chapter 2 Equipment 12

Chapter 3 Skills and Techniques 24

Chapter 4 Conservation 34

Chapter 5 Safety... 40

Features

Recipe: Venison Meatballs 11

Rifle Diagram... 15

Compound Bow Diagram 18

Essential Deer Hunting Equipment.............. 22

The Art of Stuffing Dead Stuff 32

North American Deer Species 44

Glossary 46

Read More 47

Internet Sites 47

Index.. 48

Essential content terms are highlighted and are defined at the bottom of the page where they first appear.

Chapter 1

DEER HUNTING

Learn about the history of deer hunting and kinds of deer in North America.

Deer hunting is a popular sport in North America. Deer are the most frequently hunted "big game" animals. Big game animals also include antelope, bears, buffalo, elk, and moose.

History of Deer Hunting

People have hunted deer for thousands of years. American Indians relied on deer meat for food. This meat is called venison. American Indians also made clothes and shelters from deer hides. American Indians used deer bones and antlers to make decorations and tools. They even honored deer in special ceremonies. During these events, American Indians recognized the importance of deer in their lives.

hide—animal skin

Early North American settlers also depended on deer. They ate venison and made clothing from deer hides. Settlers often sold or traded venison to stores. They also traded deer hides for items. Some settlers used deer hides to pay government taxes.

Deer Hunting Today

Today, North Americans continue to hunt deer. People hunt deer for many reasons. Many hunters eat venison from the deer they kill. They make ground venison or venison steaks. Deer hunters also hunt to spend time outdoors. Hunters observe a variety of plant and animal life. Some deer hunters enjoy spending time with friends or family members as they hunt. Other hunters enjoy hunting for a trophy deer.

A trophy deer is a male deer with very large or unusually shaped antlers. Hunters may display the mounted head of a trophy deer in their homes. Taxidermy is the process of preserving and mounting animals. For more about taxidermy, see page 32.

North American Deer

All deer share some features. Deer have narrow heads, large ears, short tails, and hooves. All deer have good senses of smell and hearing. Deer are herbivores. They eat only plants. Deer eat grasses, leaves, nuts, and fruits. They also depend on farm crops such as corn and soybeans for food.

Bucks grow new antlers during spring and summer.

Five deer species live in North America. All animals within a species share certain physical features. North American deer species include white-tailed deer, mule deer, elk, moose, and caribou.

White-Tailed and Mule Deer

White-tailed deer and mule deer are the most common North American deer species. These deer are hunted more often than other

species—a group of animals with similar features

8

North American species. Hunters use similar techniques to hunt white-tailed and mule deer.

Male white-tailed and mule deer are called bucks. Females are called does. Only bucks grow antlers. The antlers fall off each winter.

White-tailed deer live within a large area of North America. This area is called their range. The white-tailed deer's range extends from southern Canada to the southern United States. White-tailed deer are most common in the eastern half of North America.

White-tailed deer can adapt to various habitats. These include forests, swamps, fields, and prairies. White-tailed deer also live near cities and smaller towns.

Mule deer live in western North America. Their range extends south from the western Canadian provinces and territories of Yukon, British Columbia, Alberta, and Saskatchewan to western Texas. It then extends west to the Pacific coast. Mule deer prefer habitats in hilly and mountainous areas. They also live in deserts and meadows.

habitat—the natural place and conditions in which animals live

The Rut

The mating season for white-tailed and mule deer is called the rut. The rut occurs each fall. In northern areas, the rut usually begins in late October or early November. In southern areas of the United States, the rut usually begins in middle to late November. It usually lasts about two months.

The rut's season can vary depending on the weather. Cool weather early in the season can cause the rut to start a little sooner. Hot weather may delay the rut.

Deer hunting seasons occur during the rut. People are allowed to hunt during these periods in the fall. Deer often travel to look for mates during the rut. This activity makes them easier to hunt. Deer hide more often during other seasons to protect themselves from predators.

predator—an animal that lives by preying on other animals

Venison Meatballs

Serves: 3-4 Children should have adult supervision.

Ingredients:
2 eggs
$1/3$ cup (75 mL) milk
$2/3$ cup (150 mL) bread crumbs
$2/3$ cup (150 mL) Parmesan cheese
2 teaspoons (10 mL) dried parsley
1 $1/2$ teaspoons (7 mL) garlic powder
salt and pepper
1 pound (455 grams) ground venison
1 28-ounce (840 grams) can or jar of spaghetti sauce
cooked pasta

Equipment:
large bowl
spoon, egg beater,
    or automatic mixer
mixing spoon
large frying pan with cover

What You Do:
1. Combine eggs with milk in a large bowl. Mix with spoon, egg beater, or mixer.
2. Add bread crumbs, Parmesan cheese, parsley, garlic powder, and salt and pepper to egg and milk mixture. Mix these ingredients with a mixing spoon.
3. Add venison. Knead all of the ingredients with your hands and form into meatballs about the size of golf balls.
4. Brown the meatballs on all sides in frying pan over medium heat. Add spaghetti sauce.
5. Cover pan and simmer for 1 hour over low heat.
6. Serve on top of cooked pasta.

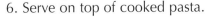

Chapter 2

EQUIPMENT

Learn about types of guns, bowhunting, and other hunting equipment.

Modern deer hunters use a variety of equipment. They use guns or bows and arrows to kill deer. Hunters also use equipment to stay safe and comfortable.

Rifles

Hunters use different guns to shoot deer. Most deer hunters use rifles. A metal case called a cartridge holds each bullet. The cartridge has powder that creates an explosive charge. When a hunter shoots, the charge pushes the bullet out of a long metal tube called the barrel. The barrel is located at the front of a gun. Deer hunters who use rifles hit targets more than 100 yards (91 meters) away.

A rifle has one of five different actions. A rifle's action loads, fires, and ejects cartridges. Actions include pump, bolt, break, lever, and semi-automatic.

Hunters must operate bolt-, break-, pump-, and lever-action rifles by hand. They load a new cartridge into these rifles after they shoot. Rifles with semi-automatic actions eject and load cartridges automatically after the shot.

Rifles come in different calibers. Caliber is the measurement of the circular barrel's diameter. Diameter is the distance from one side of a circle to the other. Caliber is often measured in thousandths of an inch. It can also be measured in millimeters.

Calibers range from about .17 to .458. Most deer hunters choose rifles that are .30 caliber or larger. Rifles that are .30 caliber have a barrel diameter of about 7.5 millimeters (.3 inch). Rifles with high calibers have more power than rifles with low calibers.

Rifles often have a scope attached to them. This viewing instrument makes the target's image appear closer. A scope helps hunters aim correctly.

It is illegal for hunters to use rifles in some locations. These areas often have many people living nearby. A bullet can travel more than 1 mile (1.6 kilometers) and hit people or objects beyond what the hunter can see.

Rifle

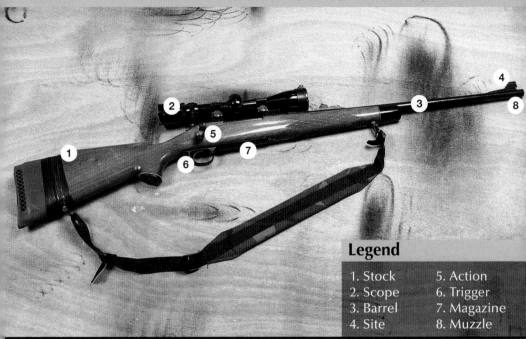

Legend

1. Stock
2. Scope
3. Barrel
4. Site
5. Action
6. Trigger
7. Magazine
8. Muzzle

Shotguns

Some deer hunters use shotguns. Shotguns can fire lead or steel shot. Shotguns can also fire a single piece of lead called a slug. Most deer hunters use slugs. A case called a shell holds the pellets or slug. Shells are usually made of plastic.

Shotguns have different gauges. The number of lead balls that fit inside a shotgun's bore determines its gauge. The bore is the barrel's inside diameter.

shot—pellets in the shell ejected by a shotgun

Guns with smaller gauge numbers are more powerful than guns with higher gauge numbers.

Together, the lead balls weigh 1 pound (.5 kilogram). For example, a 12-gauge shotgun fits 12 lead balls with a combined weight of 1 pound inside its bore.

Shotgun gauges range from .410 to 10. Gauges from smallest to largest are the .410-gauge, 28-gauge, 20-gauge, 16-gauge, 12-gauge, and 10 gauge. The .410 is the only gauge that is measured in inches. Other shotgun gauges are measured in millimeters.

Most deer hunters use 12-, 16-, or 20-gauge shotguns. Hunters consider their distance from a deer before they shoot. Hunters can use shotguns to shoot deer within a distance of about 100 yards (91 meters). Some hunters who use slugs attach scopes to their shotguns. The scopes help hunters make more accurate shots.

Muzzleloaders

Some deer hunters use muzzleloaders. Early North American settlers used these guns to shoot deer. Many hunters who use muzzleloaders enjoy the challenge of shooting deer with these guns.

Deer hunters use muzzleloaders that fire round lead balls or cone-shaped pieces of lead. Many hunters use .50 caliber muzzleloaders. But some deer hunters use them with a caliber of .54 or more.

EDGE FACT

In many states, lead shot is banned for hunting waterfowl and other birds because it can poison animals in the food chain.

Compound Bow

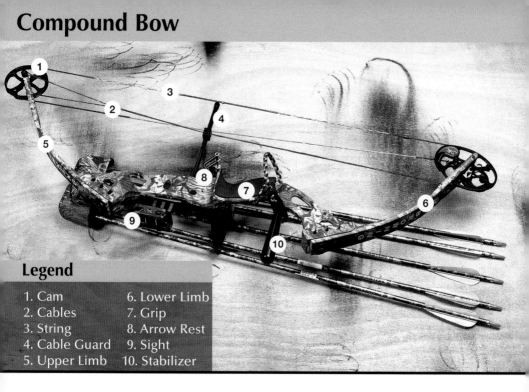

Legend

1. Cam
2. Cables
3. String
4. Cable Guard
5. Upper Limb
6. Lower Limb
7. Grip
8. Arrow Rest
9. Sight
10. Stabilizer

Hunters reload muzzleloaders by hand after each shot. This feature makes muzzleloaders slower to use than most rifles. Hunters place the piece of lead into the muzzle with gun powder. The muzzle is located at the end of a gun's barrel. The powder creates an explosive charge when the gun is fired. Hunters can shoot at deer up to about 100 yards (91 meters) away with muzzleloaders.

Bowhunting Equipment

People who bowhunt use a bow to shoot arrows at deer. Bowhunters place an arrow against a bow's string. They pull the string back and let it go. The string then snaps forward and causes the arrow to move toward its target.

Many hunters use modern compound bows. These bows reduce the amount of force needed to hold the string back. Compound bows are sometimes made of fiberglass. This strong, lightweight material is made of woven glass fibers.

Arrows are made of strong, lightweight materials. They might be a material called graphite or a metal called aluminum. Arrows usually have sharp points made of steel at one end and feathers at the other end. The feathers are made of synthetic fabrics. Feathers help keep the arrows on course as they travel.

Bowhunters must be closer to their target than hunters with guns. Most bowhunters shoot at deer less than 30 yards (28 meters) away from them. Bowhunters must be accurate. They should hit a deer in the lungs, liver, or heart.

synthetic—made by people rather than found in nature

Clothing

Deer hunters should wear clothing to keep them warm in cold weather. Hunters wear several layers of clothing. The outside layer of clothing is sometimes made of nylon. This strong material is wind- and water-resistant. Deer hunters should wear heavy coats, hats, gloves, and boots in cold weather.

Hunters should wear soft clothing to prevent noise. Deer that hear unfamiliar noises may run away or move to hidden areas. Deer hunters might also wash their hunting clothes in special soap that removes odors. Deer also avoid places where they smell unfamiliar scents.

Bowhunters should wear camouflage clothing. This clothing blends into the surroundings. It helps hunters hide from deer. Hunters who use guns should wear bright clothing. Many states and provinces require hunters to wear blaze orange or red. These colors help hunters see each other.

Hunters with guns and bowhunters usually hunt during different times to help protect hunters from injury. Hunters with guns may not see bowhunters hunting at the same time.

Bowhunters should wear camouflage clothing.

Other Equipment

Deer hunters often carry some equipment in a backpack. Hunters should bring binoculars. This viewing instrument allows hunters to see deer from a distance. Some hunters bring a compass. Deer hunters also use special deodorants to hide their scent.

Hunters should bring a first aid kit. These kits contain items such as gauze, medicine, tape, and adhesive bandages. Hunters can use a first aid kit in case of accidents or injuries.

Essential Deer Hunting Equipment

Legend

1. Gun Case
2. Compound Bow
3. Shotgun
4. Rifle
5. Arrow
6. Blaze Orange Clothing
7. Camouflage Clothing
8. Rifle Ammunition
9. Shotgun Shells
10. Binoculars

22

Hunters should have a sharp knife to field dress a deer. They cut out areas of the deer's body such as the lungs and stomach after they kill it. These parts can spoil the meat if they remain in the deer.

Some deer hunters use calls. These objects make deer sounds. The calls sound similar to the noises deer make to attract each other during the rut. Deer sometimes approach the areas where hunters use calls.

EDGE FACT

There are several different deer calls, including grunts and rattles.

Chapter 3

SKILLS AND TECHNIQUES

Learn about setting up a stand, hunting techniques, and blinds.

Hunters use various methods to hunt deer. Some hunters walk around to look for deer or walk toward deer that they see. Hunters might also wait for deer to come near them. They often use scents and calls to attract deer. They might use a lotion or spray that smells like a doe to attract bucks. Hunters can also use a call that sounds like a buck to attract does.

Deer hunters should know what times of day to find deer. White-tailed and mule deer usually eat around sunrise and before sunset. They move during periods of low light to avoid being seen by predators.

Scouting

Before hunting day, deer hunters decide where they want to hunt by scouting an area. They then learn about the area. They find out what types of deer live nearby.

Some hunters look for deer with binoculars before approaching a target.

25

Hunters also look for rubs. These scratches on tree trunks are left by bucks. Bucks grind their antlers against trees during the rut.

Hunters also look for deer tracks. White-tailed and mule deer tracks are about 2.5 to 3.5 inches (6.4 to 8.9 centimeters) long. Buck tracks are usually slightly larger than doe tracks.

Hunters also look for deer droppings. These droppings are small and oval. They are usually in piles. Each dropping is about .75 inch (1.9 centimeters) long.

Hunters look for other deer signs. They look for trails that deer regularly use. Deer often follow the same paths to and from their feeding areas. Deer trails are often between small clearings and woods. Hunters also try to discover where deer rest. They look for areas where grass or weeds are pressed to the ground.

This rub was left by a large buck during the rut.

Stand Hunting

Hunters place platforms in trees after they have scouted an area. These platforms are called stands. They are usually about 10 to 15 feet (3 to 4.6 meters) above the ground. Hunters use stands so deer cannot easily see or smell them. Deer have difficulty smelling objects above them. Hunters wait in their stands for deer to come by. Stands are placed near deer trails and deer feeding areas.

Hunters must remove stands that are on public land after the hunting season. Some hunters build permanent stands on private land. Some stands are portable. Hunters can easily move these stands to different areas.

Blind Hunting

Many hunters use natural features such as hills, trees, and weeds to hide from deer. Other hunters hide from deer in blinds. Hunters place or build these hidden shelters on the ground. Some hunters purchase blinds made of camouflage cloth from stores. Other hunters create their own blinds. Hunters often place their blinds near deer trails and feeding areas.

These hunters are hiding behind a blind, waiting for an approaching deer.

Hunters build blinds in various ways. Some place large branches around themselves. Deer hunters can also attach grasses and leaves to netting. They may attach cornstalks together and stand them up. The hunters then hide behind them.

EDGE FACT ⟶

Blinds are also used as protection from the rain and cold.

29

Deer Vital Areas

Stalking

Hunters who stalk move around often. They hope to see a deer as they travel. Hunters who stalk usually hunt alone. They walk very slowly into the wind. The wind then blows their scent away from their path. They often stop and move their head from side to side to look for deer. Hunters who stalk try to hide behind trees, ridges, or other structures.

Hunters often stalk during times of high winds or wet weather. High winds produce noise that can cover the sounds of hunters. Rain and snow help make leaves and grasses less likely to snap and crunch under hunters' feet.

The Art of Stuffing Dead Stuff

Deer Hunting—Taxidermy

Stuffing part of a carcass and hanging it on the wall—sound strange? It's actually the ancient art of taxidermy. The word taxidermy comes from the Greek, meaning "movement of the skin."

The ultimate goal of the taxidermist is to preserve an animal in a way that makes it look lifelike. Some taxidermists work for museums. Others work to preserve hunting trophies that you have to see to believe.

Most taxidermists begin their work by removing and freezing the skin of the animal. A model is created from the muscles and bones that remain. Finally, the skin is attached to the model of the animal. Sometimes glass eyes are used to make the animal look more lifelike. It's an art and a science, and it's a little creepy, too.

Chapter 4

CONSERVATION

Learn about hunting seasons, limits, and licenses.

Deer are one of the most common North American animals. Scientists estimate that the U.S. deer population is between 25 million and 30 million. But hunters still need to keep conservation in mind. They should follow state and provincial hunting regulations to help protect deer populations.

Deer Population Problems

Too few or too many deer can change an area's ecosystem. Today, many areas throughout North America have large deer populations. The deer often eat farmers' crops and cause traffic accidents.

Deer in areas with large deer populations are more likely to die than deer in less populated areas. Many of these deer are unable to find food during winter.

ecosystem—the relationship between animals and their environment

Deer hunters must know state or provincial
hunting regulations.

The deer then become weak. Weak deer are more likely to get diseases. The diseases often spread quickly in areas with large deer populations. The deer are more likely to come in contact with each other than in less populated areas.

Too few deer can also change an area's ecosystem. Deer predators may be less able to find food. These animals then may become sick or die.

Regulations

State and provincial agencies set various regulations. They examine the number of deer in certain areas. They then base their regulations on these numbers.

The limit is the number of deer a hunter is allowed to kill throughout the season. Many North American hunters can only kill one deer per season. But other hunters can kill more than two deer per season.

The length of deer hunting seasons varies according to the equipment hunters use. Many rifle and shotgun seasons begin in late October and last until mid-November.

Deer hunters with guns usually hunt at different times than bowhunters.

Bowhunting season can begin in early September and last through December or January. But bowhunters and hunters with guns usually do not hunt at the same time. Hunters who use muzzleloaders also have separate seasons from hunters who use rifles or shotguns.

Deer hunters must fill out a tag after they kill a deer.

State and provincial agencies set other regulations. Hunters need to purchase licenses to deer hunt. They need to put tags on their deer after they kill them. Deer hunters receive the tags when they purchase licenses. They mark the date they killed the deer on the tag. They also mark the location of where the deer was killed.

Young hunters often need to complete a hunter education course. This course teaches people how to safely handle guns and bowhunting equipment. It also teaches people how to identify animals before shooting them and how to handle emergencies. All state and provincial wildlife agencies offer hunter education courses.

State and provincial regulations change from year to year. Hunters must learn about the changes before each hunting season.

Chapter 5

SAFETY

Learn about gun safety and weather safety.

Deer hunters should follow safety guidelines. Hunters should keep track of weather conditions. A snow storm can cause hunters to become lost. Hunters may have difficulty seeing during heavy snowfall.

Gun Safety

Deer hunters should let other hunters know their location. They should also avoid shooting where other hunters are located. They should avoid jumping or climbing with a loaded gun. Deer hunters need to identify their target before they shoot. They should never point their gun at another person. Hunters should keep their finger off the trigger except when firing. Deer hunters must make sure to keep the safety on until they are ready to shoot.

safety—a device that prevents a gun from firing

Deer hunters should be aware of the weather conditions and their surroundings as they hunt.

41

Other Safety Concerns

Hunters should learn the weather forecast and dress properly. They should know how to use the items in their first aid kit. Safe hunters also learn about the wildlife and plants in their hunting areas. They do not bother other wildlife. They learn about harmful plants such as poison ivy. This plant can cause a skin rash.

Hunters should wear a fall-restraint device when they are in a tree stand. These harnesses strap safely around a hunter's waist and shoulders. The safety harnesses hold hunters in case of a fall.

Safe hunters always tell someone where they will be hunting. Others can then search for hunters who do not return at the expected time.

Safe deer hunters are prepared for their adventure. They try to prevent injuries and accidents. These deer hunters help make their activity safer for themselves and others.

Deer hunters should make sure they know each other's hunting locations.

EDGE FACT

When not hunting, owners should store all guns unloaded in a locked cabinet.

Mule Deer

Description: Mule deer are gray-brown. They have a narrow white tail with a black tip. Some mule deer have a white patch on their throat or chin. Mule deer are known for their large, fuzzy ears. Male mule deer weigh up to 400 pounds (181 kilograms). Females weigh up to 200 pounds (91 kilograms).

Habitat: woods, grassy areas, mountains, river valleys

Food: grasses, leaves

White-tailed Deer

Description: White-tailed deer are red-brown. Their tails are brown and white. The underside of the tail is completely white. These deer also have white patches on their nose, throat, and around their eyes. Male white-tailed deer weigh up to 300 pounds (136 kilograms). Females weigh up to 200 pounds (91 kilograms).

Habitat: woods, grassy area

Food: grasses, leaves

GLOSSARY

ecosystem (EE-ko-sis-tem)—a system of living and nonliving things in an environment

habitat (HAB-uh-tat)—the places and natural conditions in which an animal lives

hide (HYDE)—a deer's skin

predator (PRED-uh-tur)—an animal that survives by preying on other animals

safety (SAYF-tee)—a device that prevents a gun from firing

shot (SHOT)—lead or steel pellets in a shell

species (SPEE-shees)—a group of animals with similar features

synthetic (sin-THET-ik)—made by people rather than found in nature

READ MORE

Lewis, Joan. *Hunting:* Get Going! Hobbies. Chicago: Heinemann Library, 2006.

Slade, Suzanne. *Let's Go Hunting!* Adventures Outdoors. New York: PowerKids Press, 2007.

Wilson, Jef. *Hunting For Fun!* For Fun. Minneapolis: Compass Point Books, 2006

INTERNET SITES

FactHound offers a safe, fun way to find Internet sites related to this book. All of the sites on FactHound have been researched by our staff.

Here's how:

1. Visit *www.facthound.com*

2. Choose your grade level.

3. Type in this book ID **142960817X** for age-appropriate sites. You may also browse subjects by clicking on letters, or by clicking pictures and words.

4. Click on the **Fetch It** button.

FactHound will fetch the best sites for you!

INDEX